Whispers in the
Dark

Arin Burney

Presentation by *BookLeaf Publishing*

Web: www.bookleafpub.com

E-mail: info@bookleafpub.com

ISBN: 978-93-5744-975-5

First edition 2022

DEDICATION

To my Parents,

For always believing in me.

And to my great grandmother,

Who told me that everyone has a book inside them.

Jack of All Trades

Jack of All Trades
Master of None
Once I was told
That is was better than
Being a Master of One
Whether that be true or false
I can no longer tell
For what am I
But a Master of Lies
And a Jack of Nothing Else as well?

Impulsive

Think it through
Don't just go do
Advice I'd thought I'd taken
But Impulsive am I
And pause did I not
So these words I have forsaken

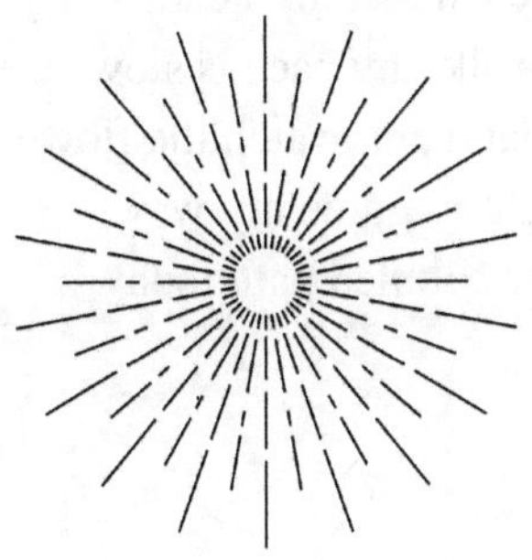

Life

Behind me lies my past
All wrapped up in a bow
Before me lies the world
To the future I will go
One and Two and Three and Four
I'll count my steps down from my door
And take the choices
One by one
Until the road is all but done
But that lies miles and miles ahead
At the place I'll rest my head
For now I walk, my pace is slow
To look around and watch the flowers grow
With sunlight to guide my way
I'll walk my cobbled path today

Dad

I remember once when I was small
You carried me so I was tall
Taller than anything around
Tall enough to reach the clouds
And when the sun it went to bed
You were there when I lay down my head
Telling stories from far away
To tomorrow; Another day
Strong and funny
Kind and wise
Always there, at my side
And when I opened my closet door
You were there waiting for me forever more
To love with all your heart
Having loved me from the very start
20 years or so have passed
And I am not at my last
Am I wiser? Am I grown?
That remains unknown
But to you, I'll always be
Your child, forever me
Wish all the love I send your way
I wish you
Happy Fathers Day

And I've tried

Before I left the golden shore
My father said to me
"Be brave and wise, through all your strife
And a better you will be"
And I've tried

I've walked a thousand miles or more
And I'll walk till the sun sets behind the shore
And each day is harder than the last
But I'll walk till the day is done

Before I stepped upon the boat
With sails of white I hope she'll float
My mother called from the shoreline coast
"Be kind of heart my dear"
And I've tried

I've walked a thousand miles or more
And I'll walk till the sun sets behind the shore
And each day is harder than the last
But I'll walk till the day is done

Before my boat she set to sail
My brothers voice carried upon the gale
"Oh sister dear, behold for you my wish,

To be happy all your life."
And I've tried

I've walked a thousand miles or more
And I'll walk till the sun sets behind the shore
And each day is harder than the last
But I'll walk till the day is done

So now as I sail across the sea
I think of the words you said to me
And I'll hold them dear for all my life
Till I see you again my dear
And I've tried

I've walked a thousand miles or more
And I'll walk till the sun sets behind the shore
And each day is harder than the last
But I'll walk till the day is done

Brave and wise I've tried to be
And kind of heart is always me
And I'm happy every day so far
So I can safely say I've tried

One

You are but one and many
Two and few
Three forgotten
And Four who knew

Five who cared
And Six who didn't
Seven stronger
But Eight is hidden

Nine created
Yet Ten destroyed
Eleven promises
Of Twelve decoyed

Thirteen is silent
Fourteen is loud
Fifteen is caring
Yet Sixteen is disavowed

Seventeen is heartless
Eighteen is kind
Nineteen is anger
And Twenty is undefined.

Sleep

My warm bed calls me from afar
I feel my eyes drifting shut
But it's morning now
So I must be awake
Even before the sun wakes up
And I won't meet my bed,
For our long awaited date
Until after the sun goes to sleep
So I'll yawn and yawn
As the day goes by
Counting the metaphorical sheep
Slowly falling asleep
Slowly falling asleep

Exotic Fruit

What makes the fruit exotic so?
I wonder why and do not know,
Is it because they are not from here
And the unknown is almost always feared?
Yet these fruits I know to find
At grocery stores that don't seem to mind
That oranges, mangos, kiwis, avocados and
more
Can never be found just outside your door?
Unless you live in heat I suppose
Is that what makes these fruits exotic so?

Choices

What makes you choose
Makes you, you
No one can change that
No one can take that
No one can turn you around
But mind what you say
Mind what you do
Mind how the world works today
For each choice that you make
Will come back around
To bring us smiles and laughter
Or sadness and frowns
You can hurt another
So quick and fast
By choices you make that last
Choices you make
Are a give and take
So watch what you choose
And watch what you do
For the world does not revolve around you.

Seven Years

They came from the Rivers
They came from the Seas
They came for our Mountains
And what lives beneath our Trees
They came armed with swords
Sharpened up to a point
We fought back with fishing rods
And bows held up taut
For seven long years war did we fight
And many of ours did lose their lives
And as the sun rose
On that fateful day
We will never surrender
But our swords were finally put away
Treaties were formed
And words were long spoken
Answered by shouts and stones that were thrown
in
This war might have ended but the battle
continued
Given to our children as a family heirloom
This fight is long winded and will never settle
For the anger, once peace,
Of the southern people
Will never be calmed as we bury our children

Who had yet to choose the life the lived in
They came from the Rivers
They came from the Seas
They came for our Mountains
And what lives beneath our Trees

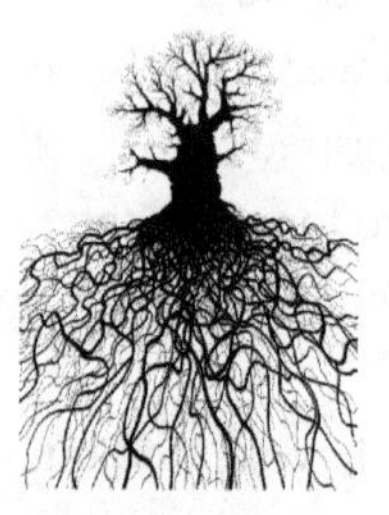

Oath of Heros

I swear upon the sun
To protect and serve everyone
I swear upon the moon
To help those less opportune
I swear upon the light
Be they human, alien or sprite
I swear upon the dark
For this oath my soul has marked
For as long as I breathe
I will help those beneath
For as long as my heart beats
I will help those that are weak
For I will be taller than the trees
And stronger than the mountains
For I will carry peace upon my shoulders
Until peace may carry itself
Of this I swear
To those who stand here
And those who stand beyond
To you I swear

Under the Willow

Down by the river
Under the Willow
Sits a Lone Ranger waiting for love
Long has he waited
Through Night and Through Day
For a lady to lighten his way

Down by the river
Under the Willow
Where Moonlight gleams down from above
Waits a young lady
Lost and Lovelorn
For a Ranger to come by her door

Down by the river
Under the willow
Where the sunlight shines
Comes the young lady
Meeting the ranger
When the light of the 'eve does arrive

Down by the river
Under the willow
With the music of wind in their ears
Dances the lady

In hand with the ranger
For many and many years

Down by the river
Under the willow
Sits the lone ranger
Waiting for love

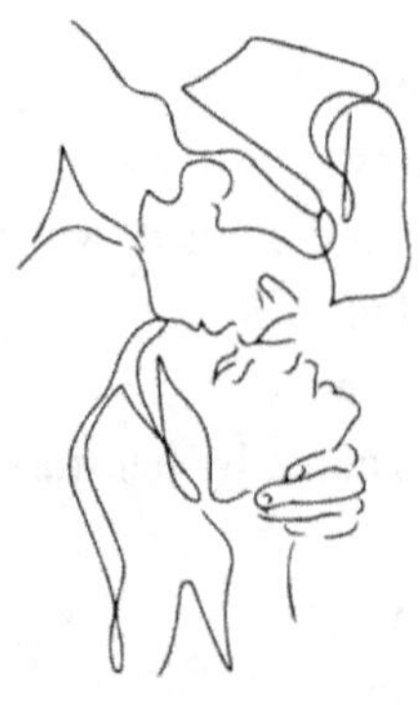

The Ranger and the Lady

Once a long long time ago
Before the dawn of hope
Lived a ranger and his lover
Beneath the willow brush

In the morning there was dancing
In the night there was song
Until the night the lady
Could not dance or sing along

In their bed she cried
As her life faded away
With her last breath
Her ranger heard her say

"Weep not for me my Ranger
Shed no tears my way
Live life to its fullest
Let your love not stay
Promise me my Rager
You will not fade away."

When her heart did stop
The wind blew one last time
The starlight lost its glimmer
And the ranger lost his mind

For many and many centuries
The Ranger lived alone
Hidden in the Willow Brush
His promise forgotten in the stone

One bright and early morning
A child found his place
Calm eyes and golden hair
A little girl with his lovers face

"Lord Ranger are you there?
I've a question for you.
The village folk call you danger
That your age is always renewed
Tell me are they lying
Tell me, is this true?"

No answer could he give
No answer did she take
So the little girl came back again
Each and every day

His lovers face she might have had
But not her form or voice

As the years flew by
He found himself with a choice

Many years had come and gone
And little girl no longer was she
Did he love her as he loved another
Or should he take to the wind and flee?

"A promise you made me Ranger
That love for me would fade
That you would continue living
Not to become a shade
This woman loves you strongly
Love is not a trade."

Five nights and Five days
Did the Ranger take to think
Of the words he heard ghosted
On that stormy fated night

His mind argued with itself
About past and future deeds
Until he came to a compromise
That satisfied both indeed

To tell her all his feelings
To bear himself anew
To hear her words and what she thought
Of his love renewed

"Lady I've come to love you
As once I loved another
Tell me do you love me
That your heart does flutter
But lie not to me Lady
Not of love or life
Should you feel different
I will take to flight"

The Lady took no time to answer
For her answer was a kiss
The stars glimmered brightly down
Upon what the Ranger had missed

"Lord Ranger I do Love you
From now and into time
I'll love you for forever
And you'll be forever mine."

And thus the Ranger danced
Through night and into day
With his Lady on his arm
He'd dance and sing his life away

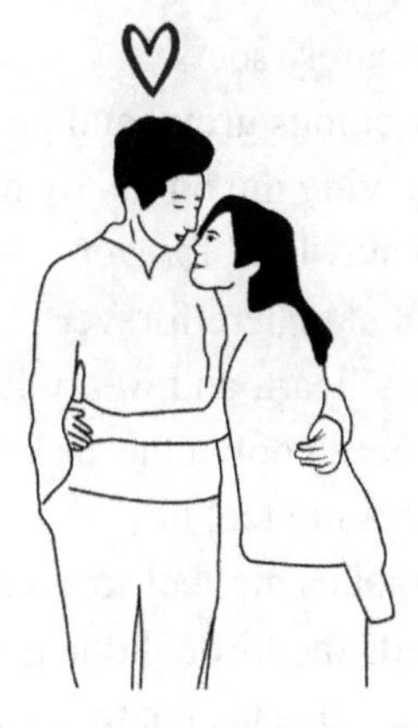

Daunting

Daunting tasks leer down at me
Throwing me to the void,
Where I can barely see
And all my demons growl and groan
My spirits leaving me on my own
But I cannot stay here forever
No, I will not stay here forever
So with weary heart, and weary feet
I stand and march down the street
Bravery makes me feel tall
Where fear makes me feel so small
Curiosity leads me through the gloom
Where arrogance leads me to my tomb
And pride is always hard to find
Sometimes bad and sometimes fine
But these tasks do not seem dark no more
Light shines in from the open door
Peace I find always helps
To keep the void at bay

After the End

It's over and done
I stare out at the horizon
From a balcony I'm not sure is mine
I dragged a world into peace
But I know it will only last for a time
And that clock is already
Ticking

I trusted him
I'd like to think he trusted me
A mentor, a friend
A traitor now, he'll always be
Lies to my face
And I'm the one to suffer
My hand, my arm, my Life
Swirls down the gutter

My love, my heart and soul
He's still here wherever I may go
My ferocious gentle Healer
He calls me
I don't see them in the mirror anymore
I see scars, and blood, and war
And all the people I couldn't
Save

But this world still needs a hero
One willing to live without a life
I'll pass this baton on
But I cannot leave this fight
So my hands might be covered in blood
But aren't a Healers always?
I'll track this bastard down
Even if it takes all my remaining days

Ending

It wasn't supposed to end this way
Blood drips down like tears

So young at the beginning
So oblivious, so naïve
My arrows flew off course
My sword never had enough force

They call me Hero
Stare at me with awe
I didn't do anything
The final blow was struck by all

7000 steps to the top
Scars of fire, now burned into my skin
My power, my voice, gone is my choice
I only feel as if I walk towards my doom

Fights a plenty
My quiver never empty
She's lied to the world, will she lie to me?
The answer is yes, a liar she will always be.

I'm scared as I call
But my voice will not waver

This battle is won
But this is no victory to savour

I call to the sky
And part hopes he will not answer
But I'm new and unknown
So his wings fly in like a dancer.

A deal is struck
It feels more like Blackmail
He brings me to him
And now all worlds hope I will not fail

I walk through the land of the dead
And I'm not sure if it's mine
I raise My sword, My bow, My magic
Our fight will last all of time

I think I won, as my blade clatters to the ground
My wounds are grievous
And I think of this life I found
Old heros surround me
It's obvious they didn't think
I'd be wounded, dying, dead
Dead in the Hall of Heros
It's so ironic I'd almost laugh
If I hadn't almost been split in half
Didn't they ask for a martyr?
A Hero to save them?

Hero's lives are tragic
I'm thankful I didn't become the villain
Our fight lasted to the end of my days
It wasn't supposed to end this way.

All Hail the Queen

All Hail the Queen
On her sunlit throne
All hope calls to her
As she guides us all to home

All Hail the Queen
Who gleams in golden sunlight
Giving way to her arrows and
Her bow she carries tight

All Hail the Queen
Who glides among the day
Our hope who will protect us
When night comes out to play

Until the morning larks
Our shield she will protect us
From who walks amidst the dark
All Hail the Queen

That shimmers through the night
Eclipsing her silver blade
Who carries the silver moonlight
All Hail the Queen

As she rides through the night alone
All shadows fear her
Upon her moonlit throne
All Hail the Queen

Little Miss Rhona

Little Rhona is at my doorstep
She came around to play
But granny says I cant play with her
And I must stay far away

Little Rhona is at my doorstep
She came with a demand
But mummy says I shouldn't speak with her
And that I must wash my hands

Little Rhona is at my doorstep
She came 'round with a task
But daddy says I cant go with her
And I must wear my mask

Little Rhona is at my doorstep
She came around to play
And I went out to play with her
And now I'll be 6 feet away

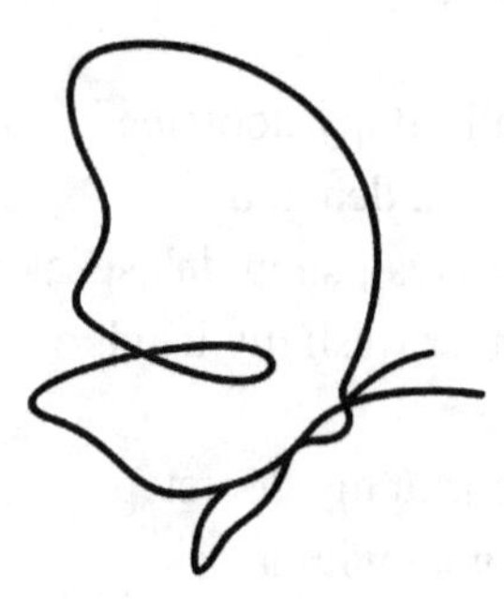

Fire

Fire, ash and burning rubble
Wind, rain and stormy skies
Plague, death and hopeless faces
This will be the end of time

Fear the one
That death does follow
Fear the two within his shadow
Fear the third who stands apart
His words will maim even the strongest heart

Fear him most
He who kills without mercy
Fear him most
He who feels no guilt
Fear him most
He who turns even the strongest of common folk
to killers

But stay your anger
Stay your rage
This may be the end of our age
But newer life will take our place
Learning from our deadly mistakes

So heed my words
And listen well
You who fear the end
Help the hurting
Heal the dying
And we may pause
This never ending wheel of time

Silence

Bright eyes gaze
Along the shore
Where water runs
And turns to gold.
From far across the lonely seas
Back again to silent trees.
They watch and wait
For dawns bright glow
To break the darkness
Only night does know.
So watch and wait,
Child, Dear
For only silence lends its ear
And only silence
Stands alone
Amid the fires
Upon a throne.
And those who stand amid these things
They listen to the silent sound
Of whispers in the dark.
So listen close
You might just hear
What your bright eyes
Have always feared.

My Heart

You are my one
You are my only
You are my love
My heart and soul
And if you find yourself quite lost
Amid the forest, deep in the frost
Know that I will find you dear
Nothing will stop me, never fear

Over mountains strong and true
From east to west
And north to south
Over trees and waters blue
I will always return to you
For you are my heart my home my soul
And I will follow where you shall go
No matter if your surely lost
I will find you no matter the cost.

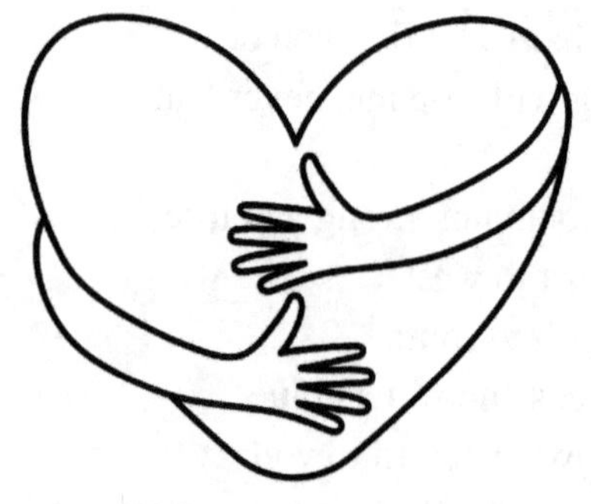